Fact Finders®

Ancient Egyptian Civilization

Ancient Egyptian
Gods
and
Goddesses

by Christopher Forest

Consultant:
Jennifer Houser Wegner, PhD
Associate Curator, Egyptian Section
Penn Museum, Pennsylvania

CAPSTONE PRESS
a capstone imprint

Fact Finder Books are published by Capstone Press,
1710 Roe Crest Drive, North Mankato, Minnesota 56003
www.capstonepub.com

Library of Congress Cataloging-in-Publication Data
Forest, Christopher.
  Ancient Egyptian gods and goddesses / by Christopher Forest.
      p. cm. — (Fact finders. Ancient Egyptian civilization)
  Summary: "Describes gods and goddesses of ancient Egypt"—Provided by publisher.
  ISBN 978-1-4296-7628-1 (library binding)
  ISBN 978-1-4296-7970-1 (paperback)
  1. Gods, Egyptian—Juvenile literature. 2. Goddesses, Egyptian—Juvenile literature.
  3. Mythology, Egyptian—Juvenile literature. I. Title. II. Series: Fact finders. Ancient
Egyptian civilization.
  BL2441.3.F67 2012
  299.3113—dc23   2011034040

Editorial Credits
Mari Bolte, editor; Juliette Peters, designer; Marcie Spence, photo researcher;
    Laura Manthe, production specialist

Photo Credits
Art Resource, N.Y.: Alfredo Dagli Orti, 6; Bridgeman Art Library International: British Museum,
London, UK, 24 (bottom), Deir el-Medina, Thebes, Egypt, 23, Egyptian National Museum, Cairo,
Egypt/Giraudon, 4, Ken Welsh, 17, The Stapleton Collection, 11, 15; Dreamstime: Indos82, 10, 12,
14, 16, 18, 24 (top), Siloto, 20, 22; Shutterstock: Andrey Burmakin, cover, BasPhoto, 21, Dudarev
Mikhail, design element, Jeffrey Liao, 9, Jose Ignacio Soto, 7, 13, Marcin Ciesielski/Sylwia Cisek, 29,
Nestor Noci, 19, Rafa Irusta, design element

Printed and bound in the USA.
1295

TABLE OF CONTENTS

Chapter 1

The Creation of the World

Ancient Egyptian myths tell of a world that was once covered in watery darkness. The darkness was known as Nun. One day, a hill grew out of the darkness. The first god, Atum, appeared on the hill. Atum created the god of air, Shu, and the goddess of moisture, Tefnut.

Nut

Geb

Ancient Egyptians believed that earthquakes were caused by Geb's laughter.

Shu and Tefnut married. They had two children. Their son, Geb was the god of the earth. Human rulers claimed to be descended from Geb. Their thrones were even known as the throne of Geb. Shu and Tefnut's daughter, Nut, was the goddess of the sky. She swallowed the sun every evening and gave birth to it every morning.

Geb and Nut married and had four children. Their sons were Osiris and Seth. Their daughters were Isis and Nephthys. Isis and Osiris married. They ruled the land with kindness. Later they had a son named Horus. He was a powerful god and became a respected ruler of Egypt.

You Married Who?

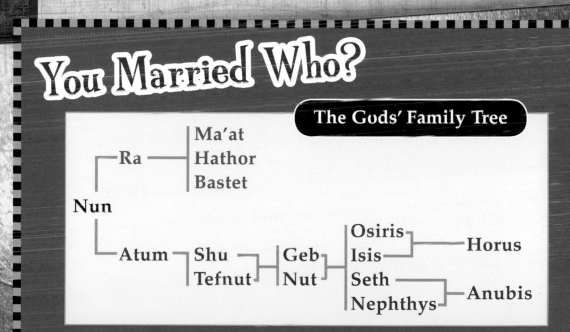

The Gods' Family Tree

The gods did not have to follow the same rules as people. This practice included rules about marriage. Egyptians believed that gods could only marry other gods. Sometimes this meant they married their siblings.

Because rulers were seen as earthly gods, the same held true for the pharaohs. While normal people did not marry their relatives, it was a common practice among Egypt's royal family.

Chapter 2

Myths and Legends

Myths and legends describe the ancient gods and goddesses of Egypt. The gods served an important role for the Egyptian people. They explained how the world worked and how people should live their lives.

Pharaohs ruled ancient Egypt for 3,000 years. The Egyptians were known for many things. They constructed pyramids as tombs for their kings. They studied mathematics and astronomy. They used the Nile River for transportation. They also used the river to water their crops. And they had an elaborate religious system that included hundreds of gods and goddesses.

myth: a story told by people in ancient times

pharaoh: a king of ancient Egypt

an Egyptian temple

Osiris Hathor Isis

The ancient Egyptians believed that the gods ruled the sky, earth, and sea. The gods controlled all life on Earth and influenced nature. They brought good harvests, storms, and drought. They also protected people from everyday dangers, such as childbirth or illness.

The people hoped the gods and goddesses would bring them a better life. Different cities selected different gods to worship. Each town had a **patron** god or goddess and a temple devoted to him or her. Without a patron, the town would be at risk for all sorts of disasters.

patron: a god who looks after a particular country or group of people

Chapter 3

Praying to the Gods and Goddesses

There were many temples devoted to the gods. The temples were made of stone because they were meant to last forever. The Egyptians believed that temples were homes to the gods and goddesses. Each day, temples had a service in the morning, afternoon, and evening. These services assured that the god would stay and protect the people.

Many of Egypt's important cities and temples were built along the Nile River.

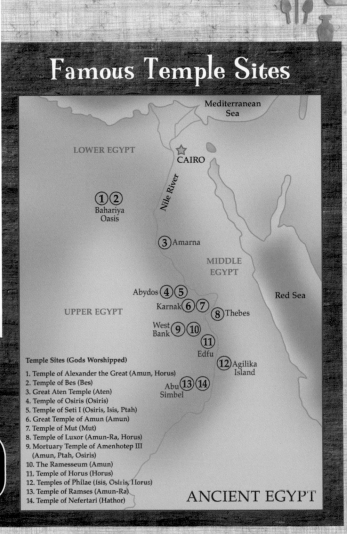

Famous Temple Sites

Mediterranean Sea

LOWER EGYPT

☆ CAIRO

Nile River

①② Bahariya Oasis

③ Amarna

MIDDLE EGYPT

Abydos ④⑤

Karnak ⑥⑦

⑧ Thebes

Red Sea

UPPER EGYPT

West Bank ⑨⑩

⑪ Edfu

⑫ Agilika Island

Abu Simbel ⑬⑭

Temple Sites (Gods Worshipped)
1. Temple of Alexander the Great (Amun, Horus)
2. Temple of Bes (Bes)
3. Great Aten Temple (Aten)
4. Temple of Osiris (Osiris)
5. Temple of Seti I (Osiris, Isis, Ptah)
6. Great Temple of Amun (Amun)
7. Temple of Mut (Mut)
8. Temple of Luxor (Amun-Ra, Horus)
9. Mortuary Temple of Amenhotep III (Amun, Ptah, Osiris)
10. The Ramesseum (Amun)
11. Temple of Horus (Horus)
12. Temples of Philae (Isis, Osiris, Horus)
13. Temple of Ramses (Amun-Ra)
14. Temple of Nefertari (Hathor)

ANCIENT EGYPT

Isis temple at Philae

Only the priests and the pharaoh were allowed inside the temple. Ordinary people got as far as the temple's courtyard on special days. They were expected to bring offerings to the gods as well as pay taxes to the temple. The offerings and taxes were used to pay the priests.

The Egyptians also worshipped gods at home. Some homes had a shrine for a chosen god. A family would have a small statue of the god. Family members left offerings of food, drink, or incense for the god.

Some gods were more popular than others. Minor gods may have been more important in one village than another. Others might be replaced as a town's patron god. The most important gods were worshipped throughout Egypt. Their names—Osiris, Isis, Horus, and others—are still known today.

Chapter 4

Osiris

Pronunciation: Oh-SY-rus
Title: god of the dead, underworld, rebirth, Nile flood, and vegetation
Appearance: a mummified man wearing a white cone-shaped headdress with feathers
Related to: Isis (wife), Horus (son), Nephthys (sister), Seth (brother)
Also called: Asar, Aser, Oser, Wesir

Osiris was one of the most respected gods. Originally, the Egyptians thought of him as an earthly ruler. He was well liked and known for being fair. He was seen as the god of fertility. The ancient Egyptians believed that Osiris caused the annual flood of the Nile River. They also believed that Osiris gave them the gift of barley, an important crop.

His brother, Seth, was jealous of Osiris' power. Seth thought he would be a better ruler. He built a magnificent chest and tricked Osiris into getting inside. Once Osiris was inside, Seth nailed the chest shut. He tossed the chest into the Nile River, leaving Osiris to die.

Osiris entering Seth's chest

While on a hunting trip, Seth found the chest. He removed Osiris's body and cut it into 14 pieces. The pieces were thrown back in the river. Seth hoped crocodiles would destroy the evidence.

Isis went on a wild search for her husband's body. She wanted to give him a proper burial. She gathered the pieces from the Nile. With the help of Anubis, the god of the **afterlife**, Isis brought Osiris back from the dead. Their son, Horus, was born during this time.

Because Osiris had died, he could not stay on Earth. He passed into the **underworld** and became the king of the dead.

afterlife: the life that begins when a person dies

underworld: resting place of spirits who had died

Chapter 5

Isis ⌐○𓁐

Pronunciation: EYE-sis
Title: goddess of life and magic
Appearance: a woman with sun and horns on her head. Sometimes shown with her hieroglyph instead.
Related to: Osiris (husband), Horus (son), Nut (mother), Geb (father)

Isis is one of the oldest goddesses of Egypt. Most ancient Egyptians worshipped her. It was believed that Isis used her magic to help people. She taught them how to farm and what they could do with the crops. She also taught them the art of healing.

She tried to help the other gods by sharing her knowledge. When a scorpion stung Horus, Isis healed him with the help of the gods Ra and Thoth.

Isis was a dedicated queen. She was known for her wisdom. She raised Horus alone after the death of her husband. Isis was seen as a link between men and gods, since pharaohs were seen as earthly versions of Horus.

Many temples were built for Isis. She was so popular that some Romans, Greeks, and other cultures worshipped her too. Temples devoted to Isis have been found as far away as Great Britain. The Temple of Isis was built by the Romans on Agilika Island in Egypt and still stands today.

Isis is also called the Mother Goddess.

FACT

Ancient Egyptians believed Isis guarded coffins and canopic jars.

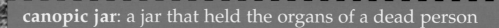

canopic jar: a jar that held the organs of a dead person

Chapter 6

Horus

Pronunciation: HOHR-uhs

Title: god of the sky, god of kingship

Appearance: a man with a falcon head

Related to: Osiris (father), Isis (mother)

Also called: Haroeris, Harpocrates, Harsiesis, Heru

Horus was one of the most important gods in ancient Egypt. He was most known for being both the protector and leader of ancient Egypt. He was also the god of hunting and war. Because of the power he represented, pharaohs were seen as Horus in human form.

Horus was the son of Osiris and Isis. His mother raised him after Seth killed Osiris. Seth feared that Horus would get revenge for his father's murder. He sent serpents to kill Horus. But Isis used her magical powers to ward off the attack.

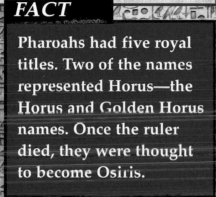

Horus was a brave fighter.

Seth's fears came true. The armies of Horus and Seth fought many battles throughout the country. After 80 years of battling, Horus and Seth squared off in the city of Edfu. There, the two enemies met in a vicious battle. Horus eventually defeated his uncle and became the new ruler of Egypt.

Eye of Horus

During his battle with Seth, Horus lost an eye. His eye was later restored. The wedjat eye, also known as the Eye of Horus, was a symbol of protection for ancient Egyptians. The god became known as a fighter for just causes.

Chapter 7

Ra

Pronunciation: RAH or RAY
Title: god of the sun
Appearance: man with a hawk head and a sun disk **headdress**
Related to: Bastet (daughter), Ma'at (daughter), Hathor/Sehkmet (daughter)
Also called: Re

Ancient Egyptians believed that Ra was the first pharaoh. Ra demanded that people follow his rules. But over time, humans stopped listening. They began to follow Apep, a giant serpent. Apep was Ra's enemy and wanted to end Ra's rule. This disappointed Ra. To solve this problem, he sent his daughter, Hathor, to destroy those who would not listen.

headdress: a decorative covering for the head

Ra died after being bitten by a cobra. Ancient Egyptians beleived that he was reborn every morning and brought the sunrise. As the day ended, he was swallowed by the goddess Nut. He spent the night in the underworld, taking the form of a man with a ram's head. He stayed in the underworld until being reborn the next morning.

Ra traveled through the underworld at the end of each day.

FACT

Ancient Egyptians thought that Ra continued his battle with Apep each day. Ra usually won the battle. It was believed that Apep won on days when there was an eclipse or a powerful storm.

Chapter 8

Hathor

Pronunciation: HATH-or
Title: goddess of birth, love, music, and dancing, and later, goddess of the dead and desert
Appearance: woman with the head of a cow, or a headdress with a sun and horns
Related to: Horus (husband, in some myths), Ra (father)
Also called: Het-Hert, Hetheru

Hathor was the goddess of women and childbirth. She was also associated with happy things, such as love and joy. She had many skills. She could cheer saddened gods with her dance. She helped inspire music. Egyptian miners prayed to her to help find riches in the eastern desert. And most Egyptians noticed her beauty.

Hathor was the daughter of the god Ra. When Ra became angry at mankind, he summoned Hathor. He ordered Hathor to destroy his enemies. Hathor took the form of a lioness and began attacking anyone who got in her way—both friends and enemies.

Egyptians called upon Hathor to predict the future. They believed that she was present at every baby's birth. It was Hathor who decided the child's fate.

a statue of Hathor at the Temple of Queen Hatshepsut

Hathor's powers grew so great that she became the Powerful One, Sekhmet the lioness. Sekhmet was a fierce fighter and a warrior goddess. Pharaohs often called upon her to lead them into battle.

To keep more people from dying, Ra tricked Sekhmet into falling asleep. When she woke, the uncontrollable urge to kill was gone.

Chapter 9

Bastet

Pronunciation: BAST-et
Title: goddess of cats, fire, the moon, pregnancy, and homes
Appearance: woman with the head of a cat (sometimes lioness)
Related to: Ra (father), Maahes (child)
Also called: Bast

Bastet was the goddess of home and pregnancy. She was thought to bring good fortune and happiness. Egyptians worshipped her in times of need or when a child was born. She was often called upon for help, and showed her gentle side in times of need.

However, Bastet had a mean streak. She was a fierce fighter. She attacked her enemies with such aggression they could rarely stop her. Her feisty side was so well known that even the pharaohs turned to her. They often asked her to protect them in battle.

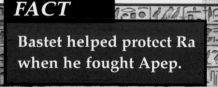

FACT

Bastet helped protect Ra when he fought Apep.

The Cats of Egypt

Cats were considered a **sacred** animal in Egypt. The cats kept the rat population down, which helped stop the spread of disease. Statues of cats were made and kept in households to honor Bastet. Cats were so sacred that they were sometimes mummified and placed in tombs.

sacred: something holy

It was believed that cats were made in the image of Bastet.

Chapter 10

Anubis

Pronunciation: ah-NOO-bis
Title: god of embalming and mummification
Appearance: human with head of a jackal
Related to: Seth (father), Nephthys (mother), Anput (wife), Kabechet (daughter)
Also called: Anpu, Ienpw, Imuet, Inpu

This jackal-headed god was associated with death and the afterlife. Priests often wore Anubis masks while embalming the dead. While some gods' appearances vary, a black jackal head always represents Anubis.

Anubis accompanied Seth as he traveled the world. After Seth was killed, Anubis decided to mummify his friend to keep his body from rotting. By preserving the body, Seth would be able to live forever. The ancient Egyptians believed that Anubis would dig up and eat any bodies that were not mummified, like a jackal.

embalming: preserving a dead body so it does not decay

mummify: to preserve a body with special salts and cloth to make it last for a very long time

Anubis guided people into the underworld. He was the final judge of a person's soul. In the Hall of Ma'at, Anubis weighed the dead person's heart on a scale. The Egyptians hoped that the scale would balance.

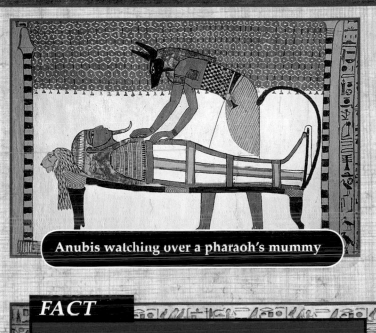

Anubis watching over a pharaoh's mummy

FACT

Anubis was a god of magic. It was believed he could predict people's futures.

Life After Death

People whose hearts balanced were sent to the realm of Osiris. They would enter a paradise called the Field of Reeds. But not all people were so fortunate. The demon Amamet sat by the scale at the Final Judgement. This demon had the head of a crocodile, the body of a lion, and the hindquarters of a hippo. He ate the hearts of the dead who were judged unworthy. Then the dead were sent to a world of fire, known as Ammit or Hetami.

Chapter 11

Ma'at

Pronunciation: mah-AHT

Title: goddess of balance, justice, and truth

Appearance: woman with a feather on her head

Related to: Ra (father)

Also called: Mat, Mayet

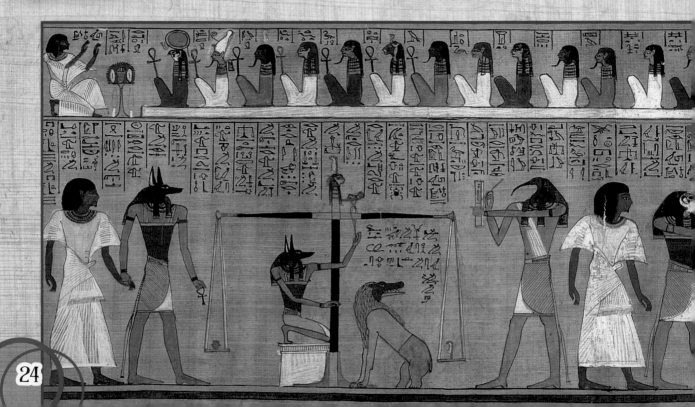

Ma'at was the goddess of balance and justice. She kept harmony on Earth by solving problems. She also made sure that justice prevailed in the land. It was believed that, without Ma'at, the universe would fall into chaos.

Pharaohs relied heavily on the goddess. In fact, they often added "Beloved of Ma'at" to their name. Pictures on temple walls show pharaohs making offerings to her. They hoped that Ma'at would bring peace to their land.

Ma'at also had a role in the afterlife. People who died were judged in the Hall of Ma'at. The goddess sat on top of a scale in the hall. She wore a crown decorated with an ostrich feather. The hearts of the dead were measured on a scale against the feather.

People who died were judged in the Hall of Ma'at.

FACT

The judge in charge of Egyptian laws was called a priest of Ma'at.

Chapter 12

Other Gods and Goddesses to Know

The world of ancient Egypt was filled with many other gods and goddesses. Some people believe there may have been around 2,000 different gods! Not every god played an important role in the daily lives of the people. Some minor gods were merely represented as ideas or symbols. But regardless of their importance, the gods helped the ancient Egyptians explain how the world worked. Some other important gods include:

Amun: King of the gods. He was similar to Zeus in Greek mythology.

Geb: God of earth. Egyptians explained earthquakes as Geb's laughter. He also allowed plants and crops to grow.

Khnum: God and creator of people and animals. He molded their forms on a potter's wheel.

Nut: Mother goddess of the sky. She helped protect the dead during their journey to the afterlife.

Sobek: A crocodile god. He was in control of the Nile River.

Seth: Son of Geb and Nut. God of chaos. He battled Osiris and Horus for rule of Egypt.

Shu: God of the air. He was believed to bring a calming influence to Egypt.

Tefnut: Goddess of rain. She was also connected with the sun and moon.

Why Did the Names of Gods Change?

Horus and Ra sometimes went by other names like Re-Horakhty or Amun-Ra. It was common for gods to have multiple names. Sometimes the Egyptians wanted to link gods who shared similar features. For example, both Ra and Atum were seen as creators. Egyptians believed Atum was one of Ra's forms and that Ra had given Atum his powers of creation. So they combined the gods into a singular form, Atum-Ra.

Other times, the names of Egyptian gods were combined with foreign gods. For example, Hermanubis was a mix of the Greek god Hermes and the Egyptian god Anubis. He became popular during Roman rule in Egypt.

Chapter 13

The End of an Empire

The world of the Egyptians included many other gods and goddesses. They were central figures in a civilization that lasted for centuries.

All of the Egyptian gods and goddesses proved important to the ancient people. They were a regular part of life and the afterlife. These gods and goddesses ruled days and nights. The people thought the gods controlled nature and created storms. They gave the Egyptians countless gifts of knowledge and food. And it was believed that they influenced the all-important Nile River. When the river flooded, the waters brought fertile soil that the Egyptians needed for their crops.

In time, the religion of ancient Egypt was replaced by other religions. The gods and goddesses slowly disappeared. But the stories of the land are told as myths and legends today. Temples devoted to the gods are still visited. The names Karnak and Luxor are particularly well-known sites. Pictures of the gods can be seen in museums on tombs, coffins, and pyramids.

Karnak Temple

The next time you hear about Osiris, Ra, or Anubis, pause for a moment. You are taking part in a tradition of storytelling that has existed for 5,000 years. Stories that made the ancient Egyptians a culture remembered to this day.

GLOSSARY

afterlife (AF-tur-life)—the life that begins when a person dies

canopic jar (kuh-NO-pik JAR)—a jar in which the ancient Egyptians preserved the organs of a dead person

eclipse (i-KLIPS)—an astronomical event in which Earth's shadow passes over the moon or the moon's shadow passes over Earth

embalm (em-BALM)—to preserve a dead body so it does not decay

headdress (HED-dress)—a decorative covering for the head

mummify (MUH-mih-fy)—to preserve a body with special salts and cloth to make it last for a very long time

myth (MITH)—a story told by people in ancient times; myths often tried to explain natural events

patron (PAY-truhn)—a god or goddess who is believed to look after a particular country or group of people

pharaoh (FAIR-oh)—a king of ancient Egypt

sacred (SAY-krid)—holy or having to do with religion

underworld (UHN-dur-wurld)—the place under the earth where ancient Egyptians believed spirits of the dead go

READ MORE

Corrick, James A. *Gritty, Stinky Ancient Egypt: The Disgusting Details about Life in Ancient Egypt*. Disgusting History. Mankato, Minn.: Capstone Press, 2011.

Deady, Kathleen W. *Ancient Egypt: Beyond the Pyramids*. Great Civilizations. Mankato, Minn.: Capstone Press, 2012.

Kennett, David. *Pharaoh: Life and Afterlife of a God*. New York: Walker & Company, 2008.

INTERNET SITES

FactHound offers a safe, fun way to find Internet sites related to this book. All of the sites on FactHound have been researched by our staff.

Here's all you do:

Visit *www.facthound.com*

Type in this code: 9781429676281

Super-cool stuff! Check out projects, games and lots more at
www.capstonekids.com

INDEX